# Crochet Your Heart

The Healing Power of Crochet

# By Pamela Davis

(The Crochet Queen)

BK Royston Publishing
P. O. Box 4321
Jeffersonville, IN 47131
502-802-5385
http://www.bkroystonpublishing.com
bkroystonpublishing@gmail.com

© Copyright – 2019

All Rights Reserved. No part of this book may be reproduced, stored in a retrieval system, or transmitted by any means without the written permission of the author.

Cover Design: Gad Savage – Elite Covers
**Cover Image © Shutterstock**

ISBN13: 978-1-946111-88-3

Printed in the United States of America

# Dedication

I want to dedicate this book to several people who have had a positive impact on my life.

The first dedication goes to my parents. If it wasn't for them hooking up, I would not exist. My father only had a second-grade education and always had a pocket full of money. My mother had a ninth-grade education and believed in pushing me towards furthering my education. I dedicate this book to both of them. They have gone on to glory, but I know they are looking down on me smiling.

I dedicate this book to my two beautiful daughters. I've always told you guys if you can dream it you can achieve it. Well guess what? I finally took my own advice, and that why this book was created to prove to you guys that nothing is impossible. Don't let NOBODY place limits on you. Your life because life is to short; so, go out and grab your success tools and hang on tight! Be sure to create several pools of income that you can access in case of emergency or just for fun.

I dedicate this book to my husband, my baby daddy, my king and my soulmate. I know we have had our ups and downs, but somehow, we manage to pull through. The thirty years I have spent with you are very memorable. I know you don't believe or even desire to make money online, but you never stopped me from trying to find my way in this ecommerce space. For that, I love you beyond the moon and back. Ronnie, you will always be my rock. I miss you baba!

# Table Of Contents

| | |
|---|---|
| Dedication | iii |
| My Early Years | 1 |
| Crocheting through Grief | 25 |
| Crocheting for Mind Clarity | 33 |
| Crochet And ADD | 39 |
| About The Author | 49 |

# My Early Years

I grew up as the baby of twelve. We were fortune enough to have both parents in the house. Being the last sibling; I was the only one that went and graduated from college, twice. My sibling didn't understand the art of hard work. They gravitated toward depending on our mother for the comfort that life had to offer. We never knew anything about public assistance until my sisters started having children of their own. Don't get me wrong there's nothing wrong with public assistance, but that's supposed to be a temporary thing until a person can get on their feet.

However, my sisters took it upon themselves to make it a lifelong journey to free monthly money. I guess that was their way of not setting higher expectation for themselves, because neither one of them graduated from high school. Since I was the youngest, I didn't look up to them for guidance. I sought guidance from our parents and other adult role models.

I remember when my father started his own waste hauling business. My father couldn't read or write, but he kept a pocket full of money. He knew all his customer's street addresses. He knew math, mainly adding and subtracting. I remember when my father would pay me and one of my sisters to help him clean out basements. We would do all the work and my father would give each of us five bucks. As a child, five bucks meant a lot to us because that was more than we had in our pockets. We never had a job that paid us money. My father was an entrepreneur before he even knew what the word meant. He was my role model and the reason why I found my way into the entrepreneurial world.

I started babysitting and shoveling snow in the neighborhood to make extra money to spend at our local store for candy. My passion for making money grew as I grew, because I believed in having multiple ways of securing extra money. When I picked up my first crochet hook back in the seventh grade, I never thought it would lead me to writing a book on the health benefits that crocheting can have on the body, mind and spirit. For me, crocheting has become my safe haven, especially since my husband died while writing this book. I had experienced loss due to both my parents and several siblings' passing, but the loss of my spouse was a different feeling. When I first got the news my husband was gone, tears didn't come from my eyes right away. My body went through and is still going through, all kinds of different emotional changes. Crocheting has helped me through the grief process of losing my husband. I remember when I got my first crochet order, I was still in grade school and my science teacher wanted me to crochet her four Christmas stockings. I had never read a pattern before, but I made those Christmas stocking between 15 to 17 inches long and about 9 to 10 inches wide. I charged her five bucks per stocking. Those stockings were professionally crocheted in the granny square stitch. I even glued white cotton at the top opening for each stocking. I wish I would have thought to take a picture, because I know I undervalued my talents as well as the cost of each stocking. That's something I'm still working on. I've gotten better at not undervaluing my talents, but I'm still a work in progress.

The word crochet dates back to the 18th century. It was originally called 'Tambour.' It eventually evolved into what the French called 'Crochet.' Once the background of the fabric was removed and stitches worked separately, crochet began to gain momentum throughout Europe in the early 1800s.

You know it's funny that I'm writing this book about the benefits that crochet can have on your health.

Whenever my husband would see me crocheting, pretty much every day he would ask me, "Aren't you tired of doing that?" And my response to him would always be, "No, it's relaxing to me." He would say, "I don't know how you sit there day in and day out looping that yarn and hook together."

I was fine. My mind was relaxed and clear of everything with the feeling of ease spreading all over my body. My husband's questions were bombarding my crochet flow and that made me nervous. Once I got the crochet hook in my hands, I instantly gained that retreat moment in my head.

My love of crocheting developed back in the 7th grade, that's when Home Economics was part of the school's curriculum. The semester started with cooking and sewing. It progressed to other crafts like plastic canvas, latch hook, macramé, crocheting & knitting. I gravitated towards crochet more than any other craft. I never knew you could use a hook and some yarn to create a masterpiece.

When I first got the hook and yarn in my hand, I gripped it so tight my chain of 10 looked like a chain of 4 stitches. All you crocheters know that in order to produce quality work, you must loosen your grip. Because once you reach the end of the row, you turn your work and continue crocheting into each of the foundation chains.

It took me three or four tries before I loosened my grip and got the rhythm and technique of crochet. Once I did, I took off like a crocheting rocket. Of course, that doesn't mean I designed patterns or started building my crochet business, that was years down the road.

When I first started to crochet, I was nervous and didn't understand that I needed to relax to have proper form with my stitches. Now I'm known as the 'Crochet Queen' with thirty-eight years under my belt hooking around with different type of yarns and stitches. Who knew that twelve-year-old girl back in the seventh grade would create a business out of her new-found craft? 'Not I,' said the duck?

I've always been a curious child wanting to try new things that I had never done before. That's probably why home economics became one of my favorite classes. That was a time where I could express myself through creativity. Once I got the crochet hook in my hands the possibilities were endless. My creative juices start to flow and did not stop until I get my project completed to my satisfaction.

Of course, my creative juices really start to flow when I walk in the yarn section of the fabric store. I can spend hours just looking and feeling all the different colors and textures of yarns. I feel so at ease when I walk in the yarn section. My creative side takes over, because I know the possibilities are endless.

I never knew about all the health benefits crocheting can have on the body, mind and spirt until I stopped for a while. I used to suffer from bad anxiety that kept me up at night. My husband would get up with me just to make sure I was alright. It felt like there was an elephant standing on my chest. I couldn't lay down or even sit in the chair. The only thing that helped was walking back and forward in my house from one room to the next. Prior to my anxiety attacks, I had been crocheting for years, but I put it on the back burner after I had my children.

With the birth of each child, our bodies go through different changes, some good and some bad. The strange part about my anxiety was it didn't develop until both of my children were school age. I guess my hormones were on a break and decided to kick in when they felt like it. But once I picked back up my craft, I noticed that my anxiety went away. It's the repetitious hand

and eye coordination with the back and forward movements.

Crocheting controls the central mind to a restful pace when you're dealing with anxiety of redundant feelings. By keeping your mind and hands busy, you control what can and can't invade your mind space. Individuals with Obsessive Compulsive Disorder and eating disorders can benefit from crochet because the counting motion soothes the mind to a normal state and distract from negative feelings and actions on the body and mind. Anxiety is panic attacks that can be terrifying. It comes with the gripping feeling over the body and mind with fear of helplessness that can last 3-7 minutes but seems like hours of agony pain. By utilizing the technique of a hook and yarn, you are able to control those annoying feelings and/or limit them.

I have a sister who suffers from depression. She also has a drug addiction as well. I remember her telling me that she and my other two older siblings were taken from the house when they were young at least once a month and given shots. I asked her what the shots was for and she never knew, but "Our parents okayed it," She said. It's funny now that I think about it; each one of my siblings that received the shot abused drugs and alcohol. I read an article a long time ago that said, 'if a person drank one Alcoholic beverage a month, they were classified as an alcoholic.' Now that was a long-time ago, but I find that hard to believe that one alcoholic beverage a month can classify someone as being an alcoholic. My whole family abused alcohol and drugs in one form or another. Of course, the abuse started with my parents. They were daily alcohol drinkers; however, they never abused illegal drugs.

Our parents both worked outside the home for financial compensation. My siblings did not ascribe to the same work ethic. It was important for me however, to exclude myself from their type of thinking and work ethic. I can remember when my oldest sister came home and told our mother that she was pregnant with her first child. My mother's words to her were, "Quit your job and move back home." That was the worst advice my mother could have ever given my sister, because she became dependent on my mother and others for her lifestyle. I understand that everyone chooses their own destiny in life, but one can only choose to be great if they have ambition to be great. My siblings chose to depend on government assistance and was upset because I chose the route to be dependent on myself. Crocheting has lead me down the road to freedom and success.

Crocheting can help relieve depression. Did you guys know that when you crochet the brain releases a chemical called serotonin, it's a natural anti-depressant? Our bodies are a natural entity, so why not provide it with natural techniques and supplements? Don't get me wrong, I'm not advocating that you stop taking your medications prescribed by your doctors. I am advocating that you look into alternative means to help heal the body naturally. And what better way than crochet. You can heal the body and learn a technique that you can take with you for the rest of your life.

By learning to crochet, you're actively taking steps to take care of yourself. There are numerous studies that document the health benefits crocheting/knitting can have on your body, mind and spirit. I know for me when I was suffering from anxiety, it took me years of research to learn how the repetitive crochet technique can help to cure my anxiety. I never thought a hook and yarn could have a positive effect on the body in a positive manner.

I can remember a time growing up being afraid to speak my mind, afraid to have confident in myself and afraid to question others' opinions. I was never sure of myself. I never had the self-esteem that made me the woman I am today. I remember when my two older sisters would talk me and my other sister into babysitting their children. They would tell us they would pay us ten dollars while they go out and party. Payday never came for our services and we never questioned them about it. They pulled that stunt on us a few times before we realized that there would never be any compensation.

It took me a long time to develop my own voice, the voice that said what I meant and meant what I said. That's what crochet can do for you. It builds your self-esteem as well as your self-worth. It empowers you with a voice that can be heard for miles around. You will absorb the confidence you need with every stitch performed. You can create beauty within yourself all while mastering your love of crochet. The self-expression through one stitch at a time is amazing. You are able to build a foundation that no one will tear down unless you allow them.

Crocheting can help you see the beauty within you. It allows you to be in the driver's seat, because you control the stop and go practice that crocheting will bring into your life. Crocheting is like a retreat in your head, it's like your own mental vacation that's how relaxing it can be. One should never look to someone else to build their self-esteem, because they will let you down at every turn. However, by using your skills you gain through crochet, the completed projects will build your self-esteem for you. Because people will begin to rave about your talents and that will build your confidence levels to newer highest.

I have talked numerous times on my live broadcast about the positive effects crochet has with early onset signs of Alzheimer's. Studies have showed that crochet can reduce the Alzheimer's disease by 30-50%. The repetitive action helps keep the mind focused. In the early stages of the disease, if the patient learns a new skill that's difficult, it can energize the brain cells and support the negative affects Alzheimer's has on the human brain. Crocheting allows the mind to focus on different stitches for the project, and it helps the patient with attention to detail for proper counting techniques.

Crocheting improves hand and eye coordination. It allows the body to build endurance that creates a wall against Alzheimer's. Crocheting can also be calming for those people who are already facing signs of dementia. There was a study done on females between the ages of 40-61 who said that when they crochet it makes them feel happy and it helps with their memory. Crochet is known for reducing stress. Whenever stress levels in the body are elevated, it leaves room for all kinds of bad things to happen in the body, mind and spirit. Just one hour of crocheting can help control stress levels that can support overall body health.

Let's face it, stress can cause all kinds of illness in our bodies. That's why it is helpful to have a skill like crochet that can occupy your mind for overall body health. Doing something as simple as hooking different stitches together for mind control is very beneficial due to the early detection of many illnesses that might affect the body. Don't get me wrong, I am not advocating that you stop taking any medication your doctor might have you on, because I am not a medical doctor. But if you can utilize a skill like crochet that can help improve your memory, why not?

# Crocheting Through Grief

While I was writing this book, I experienced a devasting loss. My partner of thirty years died unexpectedly. I don't understand how I went from talking to him about groceries, to sending him to the store, he actually went to two stores to calling 911 for emergency assistance. You know it's really true what they say, 'Be careful what you say to someone, because it just might be the last thing you say to that person.'

Crocheting helps solve a lot of health issues. Well I'm here to tell you, it's true. Because when I first realized that I would not see my soulmate again, everything stopped. I didn't want to crochet. I couldn't sleep. And every time I talked about what happened to him, my chest would start to hurt. The same night when I came home from the hospital, I was peeing every 5 minutes. My butt was sweating like I had been exercising really hard.

My body was crying due to the devasting loss I had experienced. I'd experienced death in my family before and my reaction to it was pretty much the same. But with my husband's death, it was very different. On the way to the hospital, we got stopped by a train. I told my daughters that this wasn't good, something was really wrong. I was right. Because by the time we got to the hospital, they said his heart rate was all over the place. When he left the house, he had a faint pulse. They shocked my husband five times before leaving the house. I guess that's how they were able to get a faint pulse.

If someone had told me that on March 24, 2019 that my husband was going to die that day, I would have cursed them out and got the hell away from them. My husband was a healthy man. He had high blood pressure that was controlled by medication, diet and exercise. He knew just about every herbal cure for whatever symptom you had. It's still hard to believe that someone who advocated for everyone else's health; when it came to his health, ended up losing his life. I'm still having trouble wrapping my head around the situation.

Once I realized that my husband's death was starting to affect my body, I knew I needed to do something. So, I picked up my trusty crochet hook and yarn and started working on my incomplete projects. Oddly enough, it helped. I noticed when I talked about what happened to him, my chest didn't hurt. I wasn't peeing every five minutes and my butt wasn't sweating anymore. So, there is relief at the end of each stitch I made during those difficult times for me and my family.

I didn't pick up my crochet hook to forget about my husband. I picked up my crochet hook because my body needed some type of relief. Like I said before, I've lost loved ones, but my husband's death really affected me in a negative way. I have experienced death before, but I never experienced the effects that his death was having on my body. So that was really scary to me. I even thought maybe this is how I can be with him. But once I looked into my children's eyes, I knew I had made the right decision by picking up the crochet hook and yarn for therapeutic support during this devasting time.

What I want you guys to take from this book, is that anything is attainable. Don't sit back and let life pass you by. Stop procrastinating with your gifts and talents. I've always wanted to retire with my husband and buy him a brand-new truck. Now, I will never get to do that because I let procrastination hold me hostage. I pray that I will never allow procrastination and fear to hold me back ever again! It's one thing when you sit back and crochet behind the scenes and never project your voice for the common good. By not sharing your gifts with the rest of the world, you are missing out on your blessings that God has given you for a reason. That reason was not to hide behind closed doors. I would have never thought about crocheting being therapeutic in the grieving process. Within all the live videos, I've talked about how crocheting can help with body, mind and spirit. Well grief is a body, mind and spiritual thing. Crocheting provides clarity in your life. There's no right or wrong way to grieve, it affects everyone differently.

May 24, 2019 marked two months since my husband died. That

was a difficult day for me and the girls. I noticed when I would talk about my husband, my chest started hurting just like it did when it first happened. Every time I think I'm adjusting to the new normal, my love and emotional state take over, and I find myself crying and yearning for his voice and touch. Now I know how my mother felt when my father died all those years ago. I still feel like we are married. I don't feel like a widow. The only difference is I can't see him, touch him or hear him.

# Crocheting for Mind Clarity

When I pick up my crochet hook and yarn, it's like a retreat in my head. I'm able to sit and find clarity with my thoughts. It always allows me to stay alert and focus on the task at hand. When a person crochets, their mind is at ease and their thoughts are clearer, which make life easier when multi-tasking like most women do. I like to describe crocheting as mind cleaning because your thoughts become clear, and you gain perspective in your life. Many people crochet because it helps them to relax their mind and inner being. Individuals who immerse themselves in the craft of crochet, find themselves at peace with life's events.

I know when my husband died, I couldn't think. I couldn't even talk about what happened to him without experiencing pain. His death was affecting my body, so I had to pick up my yarn and hook to get some kind of new normal because my normal life was my husband. We met each other when I was nineteen years old, and he was twenty-nine years old. I grew up with my husband. I didn't know any other man. Ron had everything I ever needed in a man. He pulled me out of debt multiple times. The fiscal year 2019 when the government shutdown, he had the money for the mortgage payment and jeep payment. Talk about a standup man for his family, even though he would complain about it, he would do it no matter what.

So, crochet brought me back from this devasting loss of my husband. Now don't get me wrong, I still have my moments when I find myself getting choked up and can't talk because I miss him so much. By me picking up my crochet hook and yarn, it allows me to breath, focus and get perspective on life's devasting moments. Crochet has been a lifeline for me to keep my sanity. I turn to crochet when I feel stressed out which sometimes is pretty much every day. There's a book in all of us. This crochet your heart book has been in me for years and I didn't even know it.

Tap into your strengths. We all have something that we are passionate about. Why not turn that passion into legacy for you and your family?

I can remember when I first contracted with my coach back on February 01, 2018. She's the type of coach that believes in sharing her platform with her clients. She is always hosting conferences where she invites her mentees to speak on stage. I haven't spoken on her stage **<u>YET,</u>** **<u>but</u>** guess what? I plan to. Because I thought public speaking was the scariest thing, but when I had to bury my soulmate on April 6, 2019, that was the scariest and most difficult thing I have had to do in life.

## Crochet and ADD

Attention deficit disorder is a touchy subject for many people who suffer from it; however, it is something that can be controlled one stitch at a time. I know that individuals never want to admit they have a disorder, but if you really think about it, we all have some kind of disorder. I know for me, sometimes it's hard for me to concentrate when I'm reading a book. Because my mind starts wandering, and I will read the same sentence twice before I realize it.

I notice when crocheting, I'm extra careful with each stitch and pay close attention to details, especially if I am reading from a pattern. Even if I get interrupted, I'm able to go back and figure out quickly where I left off. I notice that I can retain the stitches in my mind more so than reading a book. Crochet provides the mind with clarity and focus so that you can produce your best work. I named this book 'Crochet Your Heart.' As we all know that the heart is a muscle and it requires exercise and healthy nutrition. Although crochet is a physical hand sport, there are so many other benefits it has on the body like concentration.

I hate the fact that when I try to concentrate on something other than crochet, my mind starts to wander from the task that I'm working on. I believe that everyone has a bit of attention deficit disorder, but they are too embarrassed to admit it. There are tricks you can do to keep your mind focused on each task you want to accomplish. Things like deep breathing, soaking in warm water, listening to soothing music, practicing mindful meditation and of course, crocheting. I remember when I was in college studying for a test, I would create ways to help me remember the study material. I would write the answers down several times or remember by using a rhyming method for each answer that related to the test. When I lost my soulmate on March 24,

2019, before his death, I thought writing and public speaking was the hardest thing in life. That's not true because losing my husband and planning his funeral was the most difficult thing I had to do in my life. I've experienced death because I lost my father in 1995, my brother in 2009, my mother in 2017 and one of my sister's in 2018. I was upset about their deaths, but losing my partner and my lover is a different kind of feeling and loss. Before his death, I would crochet everyday nonstop. After his death, I didn't want to crochet.

Every time I talk about how it happened, my whole body would start to cry. I had to crochet to heal my heart, because it had been broken by the unexpected loss of my husband. I used to tell myself that if I can build a successful crochet business, I can retire the both of us, so we could live the life that God meant for us to live and stop living paycheck to paycheck.

Since I let procrastination take over, I won't be able to do those things for him because he has gone on to glory. Procrastination will leave you broke, stuck and empty inside because you never get to accomplish your dreams. Don't let nobody or nothing stand in your way of destiny, because greatness is around the corner for everyone. You just have to make the right turn, reach out, grab it and hang on tight for the ride. This book been a healing tool for me. The person I loved the most won't get to read this book because he is no longer with me, but I believe he's with me in spirit. It took me a long time before I could structure a proper sentence, and now I'm writing a book. My point is: Don't put limits on yourself. Get out of your own way and write down your thoughts and pain, because there is power in words. There's healing power in every technique, like crochet and writing. Crochet helps to center your thoughts. Crochet relaxes you and it provides mind clarity so you can produce quality work. All the qualities and colors of yarn, the feeling of the items that you're creating and the stunning movements of each stitch can get you one day closer to mind clarity which is what we all need some days. The pain of losing my husband was and still is unlike anything I have ever experienced. Just to find some kind of relief was hard for me, because I felt like I was losing him all over again. After being with someone for thirty years, you eat, sleep and dream about that person because the two of you became one. When I got to the point that I was at a loss for words, my crafting has helped me cope with the loss and provide me with mental clarity.

I've always been the type of person that has multiple crochet projects in the works. And I'm still that person with the same multiple projects, but the difference is I can see the end in sight. Since the death of my husband, I look at each completed project as him praising me for a job well done as he would always do. He was my biggest supporter when it came to my crochet work. He named my first crochet pattern. He would support me by buying crochet hooks. Of course, he would always tell me to rest my hands, because he didn't want me to get burned out with crocheting too much.

I always thought I would have my husband by my side when I released my first book, but in essence, he is by my side, I just can't see or touch him. There really is healing in crocheting. Our baby girl recently learned to crochet. Since the death of her father, she's been experiencing a lot of anxiety. She shared with me that crocheting actually helps with her anxiety so she can sleep at night. Her father has always told her, "That if you pick up half of what your mother knows, you will always be able to have success in your life." This 'Crochet

Your Heart' book is my own platform of personal healing. Because I've always told my children, "If you can dream it, you can achieve it." So, I started taking my own advice by completing things I started. Because as a fifty-year-old adult, I want to live my life to the fullest.

## About The Author

Pamela Davis is an entrepreneur working toward building her Krochet Kousin empire. In her spare time, she loves to spend it with her two beautiful daughters and take family cruises.

For 18 years, she has worked as a building management specialist with GSA.

Pamela owns Krochet Kousin business and to find out more about Pamela Davis on Social Media visit krochet cousin on Instagram and crochet cousin on Facebook or follow her on social media on or email her at krochetkousin2019@yahoo.com.

www.ingramcontent.com/pod-product-compliance
Lightning Source LLC
Chambersburg PA
CBHW031216090426
42736CB00009B/936